17.25

COLDPLAY · PARACHUTES

CW00806419

Wise Publications
London/New York/Sydney/Paris/Copenhagen/Madrid/Tokyo

Exclusive distributors:
Music Sales Limited
8/9 Frith Street, London W1D 3JB, England.

Music Sales Pty Limited
120 Rothschild Avenue, Rosebery, NSW 2018, Australia.

Order No.AM968264
ISBN 0-7119-8587-1
This book © Copyright 2000 by Wise Publications.

Music arranged by Matt Cowe.
Music engraved by Paul Ewers Music Design.

Printed in the United Kingdom by
Caligraving Limited, Thetford, Norfolk.

Your Guarantee of Quality:
As publishers, we strive to produce every book to the highest commercial standards.
The music has been freshly engraved and, whilst endeavouring
to retain the original running order of the recorded album, the book has been carefully
designed to minimise awkward page turns and to make playing from it a real pleasure.
Particular care has been given to specifying acid-free, neutral-sized
paper made from pulps which have not been elemental chlorine bleached.
This pulp is from farmed sustainable forests and
was produced with special regard for the environment.
Throughout, the printing and binding have been planned to ensure a sturdy,
attractive publication which should give years of enjoyment.
If your copy fails to meet our high standards, please inform us and we will gladly replace it.

Music Sales' complete catalogue describes thousands of titles and
is available in full colour sections by subject, direct from Music Sales Limited.
Please state your areas of interest and send a cheque/postal order for £1.50 for postage to:
Music Sales Limited, Newmarket Road, Bury St. Edmunds, Suffolk IP33 3YB.

www.musicsales.com

GUITAR TABLATURE EXPLAINED

Guitar music can be notated three different ways: on a musical stave, in tablature, and in rhythm slashes

RHYTHM SLASHES are written above the stave. Strum chords in the rhythm indicated. Round noteheads indicate single notes.

THE MUSICAL STAVE shows pitches and rhythms and is divided by lines into bars. Pitches are named after the first seven letters of the alphabet.

TABLATURE graphically represents the guitar fingerboard. Each horizontal line represents a string, and each number represents a fret.

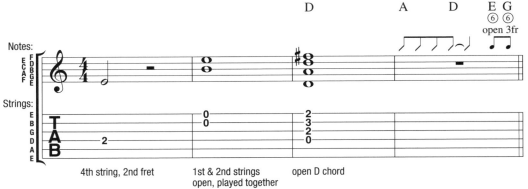

4th string, 2nd fret   1st & 2nd strings open, played together   open D chord

DEFINITIONS FOR SPECIAL GUITAR NOTATION

SEMI-TONE BEND: Strike the note and bend up a semi-tone (1/2 step).

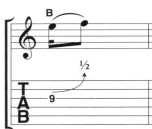

WHOLE-TONE BEND: Strike the note and bend up a whole-tone (whole step).

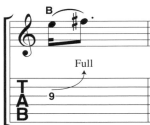

GRACE NOTE BEND: Strike the note and bend as indicated. Play the first note as quickly as possible.

QUARTER-TONE BEND: Strike the note and bend up a 1/4 step.

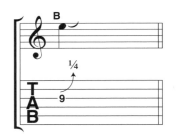

BEND & RELEASE: Strike the note and bend up as indicated, then release back to the original note.

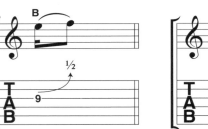

COMPOUND BEND & RELEASE: Strike the note and bend up and down in the rhythm indicated.

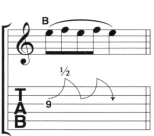

PRE-BEND: Bend the note as indicated, then strike it.

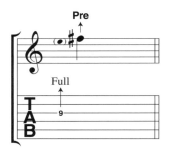

PRE-BEND & RELEASE: Bend the note as indicated. Strike it and release the note back to the original pitch.

UNISON BEND: Strike the two notes simultaneously and bend the lower note up to the pitch of the higher.

BEND & RESTRIKE: Strike the note and bend as indicated then restrike the string where the symbol occurs.

BEND, HOLD AND RELEASE: Same as bend and release but hold the bend for the duration of the tie.

BEND AND TAP: Bend the note as indicated and tap the higher fret while still holding the bend.

VIBRATO: The string is vibrated by rapidly bending and releasing the note with the fretting hand.

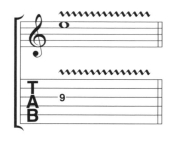

HAMMER-ON: Strike the first (lower) note with one finger, then sound the higher note (on the same string) with another finger by fretting it without picking.

PULL-OFF: Place both fingers on the notes to be sounded, Strike the first note and without picking, pull the finger off to sound the second (lower) note.

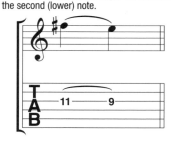

LEGATO SLIDE (GLISS): Strike the first note and then slide the same fret-hand finger up or down to the second note. The second note is not struck.

NOTE: The speed of any bend is indicated by the music notation and tempo.

SHIFT SLIDE (GLISS & RESTRIKE): Same as legato slide, except the second note is struck.

TRILL: Very rapidly alternate between the notes indicated by continuously hammering on and pulling off.

TAPPING: Hammer ("tap") the fret indicated with the pick-hand index or middle finger and pull off to the note fretted by the fret hand.

PICK SCRAPE: The edge of the pick is rubbed down (or up) the string, producing a scratchy sound.

MUFFLED STRINGS: A percussive sound is produced by laying the fret hand across the string(s) without depressing, and striking them with the pick hand.

NATURAL HARMONIC: Strike the note while the fret-hand lightly touches the string directly over the fret indicated.

PINCH HARMONIC: The note is fretted normally and a harmonic is produced by adding the edge of the thumb or the tip of the index finger of the pick hand to the normal pick attack.

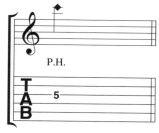

HARP HARMONIC: The note is fretted normally and a harmonic is produced by gently resting the pick hand's index finger directly above the indicated fret (in parentheses) while the pick hand's thumb or pick assists by plucking the appropriate string.

PALM MUTING: The note is partially muted by the pick hand lightly touching the string(s) just before the bridge.

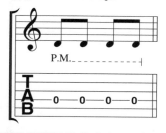

RAKE: Drag the pick across the strings indicated with a single motion.

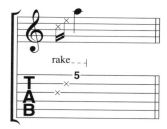

TREMOLO PICKING: The note is picked as rapidly and continuously as possible.

ARPEGGIATE: Play the notes of the chord indicated by quickly rolling them from bottom to top.

SWEEP PICKING: Rhythmic downstroke and/or upstroke motion across the strings.

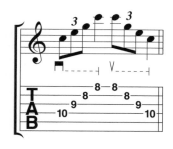

VIBRATO DIVE BAR AND RETURN: The pitch of the note or chord is dropped a specific number of steps (in rhythm) then returned to the original pitch.

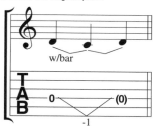

VIBRATO BAR SCOOP: Depress the bar just before striking the note, then quickly release the bar.

VIBRATO BAR DIP: Strike the note and then immediately drop a specific number of steps, then release back to the original pitch.

ADDITIONAL MUSICAL DEFINITIONS

(accent)	•	Accentuate note (play it louder).
(accent)	•	Accentuate note with great intensity.
(staccato)	•	Shorten time value of note.
	•	Downstroke
V	•	Upstroke

D.%. al Coda

• Go back to the sign (%), then play until the bar marked *To Coda* ⊕ then skip to the section marked ⊕ *Coda*.

D.C. al Fine

• Go back to the beginning of the song and play until the bar marked *Fine* (end).

tacet

• Instrument is silent (drops out).

• Repeat bars between signs.

1.	2.

• When a repeated section has different endings, play the first ending only the first time and the second ending only the second time.

NOTE: Tablature numbers in parentheses mean:
1. The note is sustained, but a new articulation (such as hammer on or slide) begins.
2. A note may be fretted but not necessarily played.

DON'T PANIC

Words & Music by Guy Berryman, Jon Buckland, Will Champion & Chris Martin

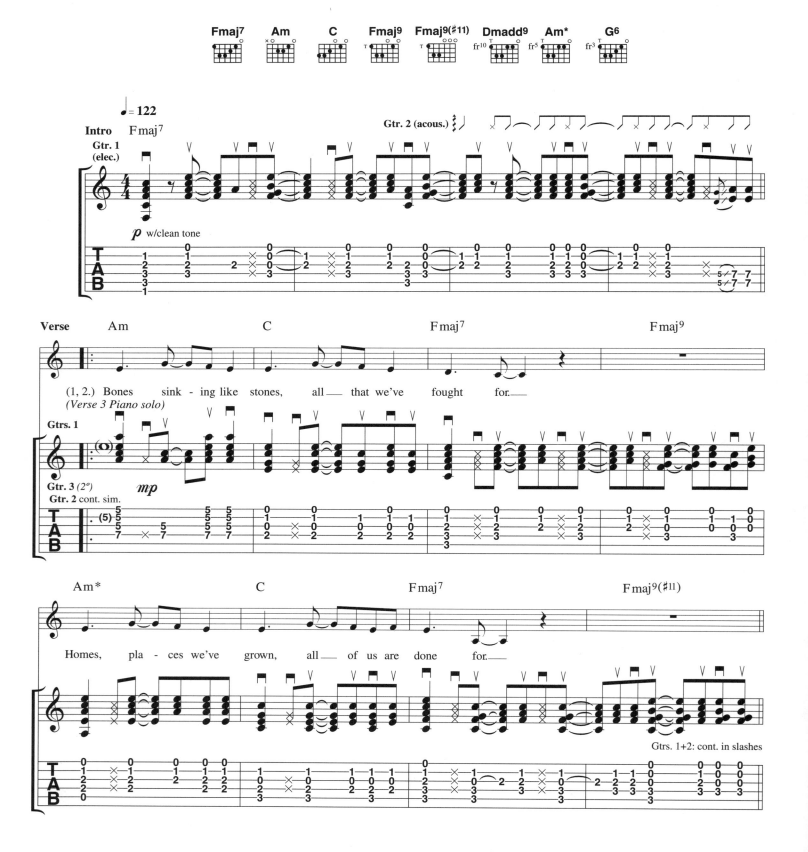

8

SHIVER

Words & Music by Guy Berryman, Jon Buckland, Will Champion & Chris Martin

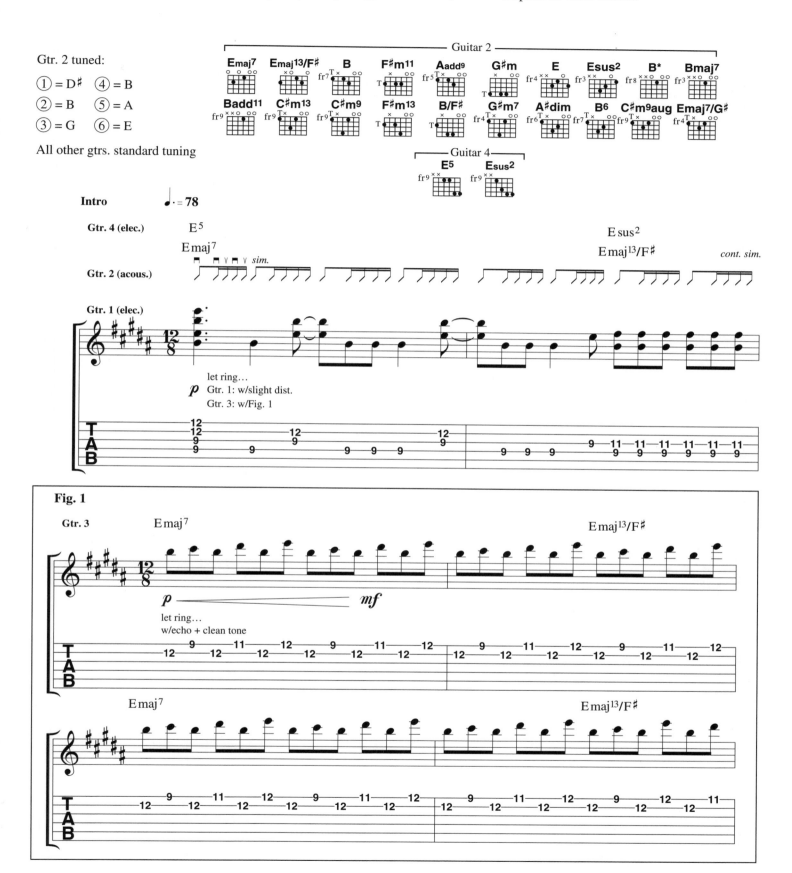

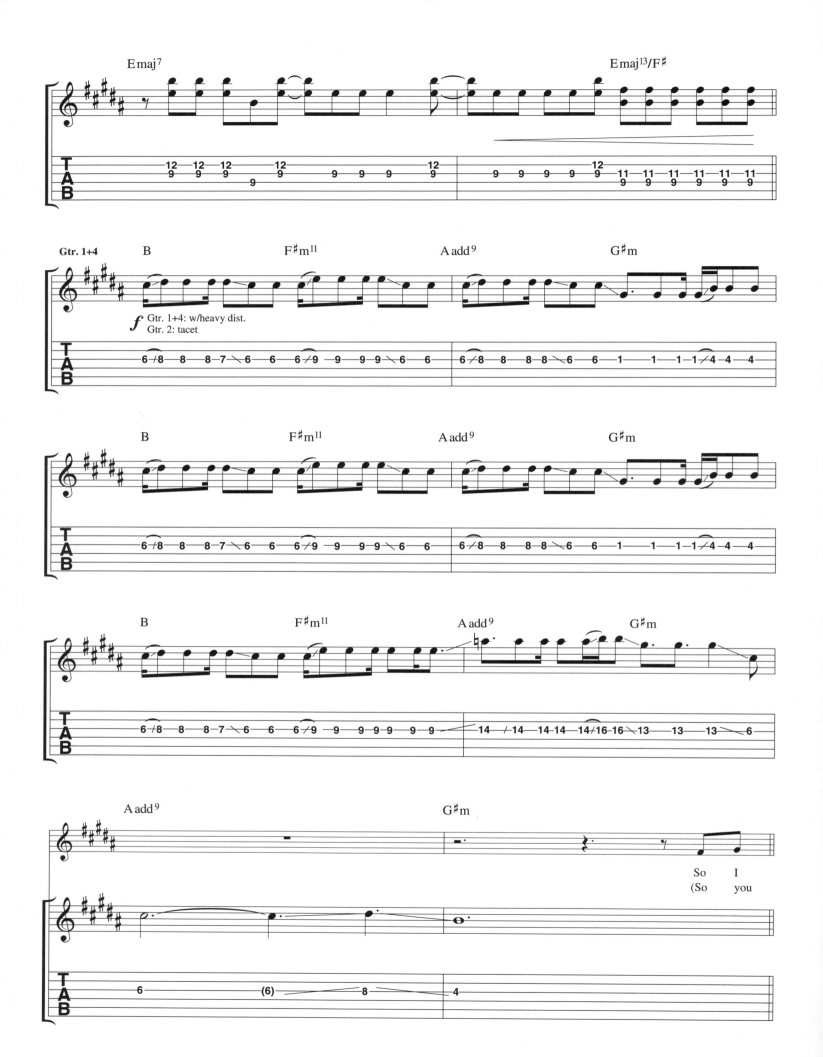

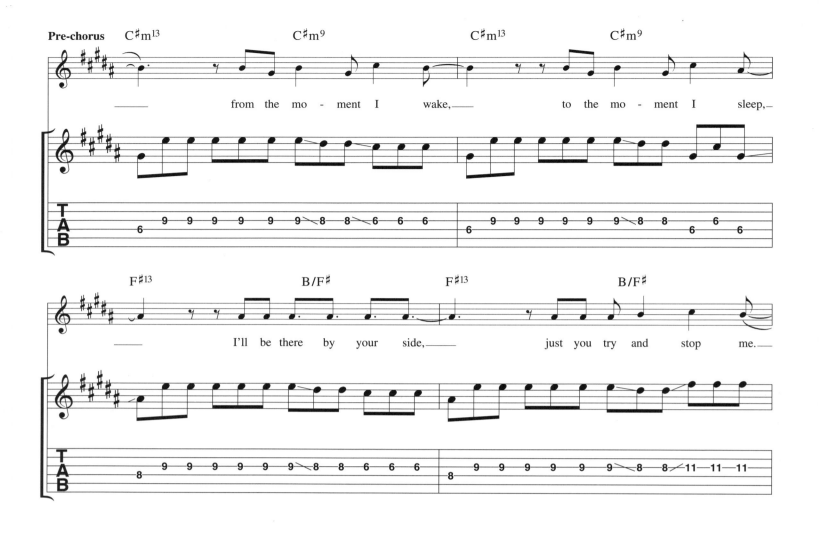

I'll be wait-ing in line_____ just to see if you_____ care._____

Oh_____ whoa._____

Did you want me to change,_____ well I'd change for good,

2° Gtr. 3: w/Fig. 3 (x3)

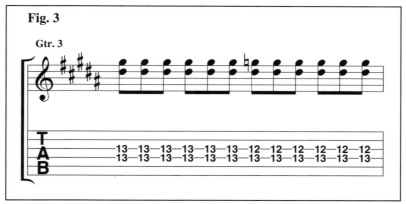

Fig. 3

Gtr. 3

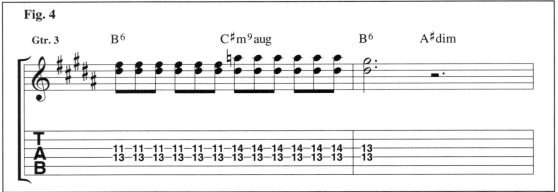

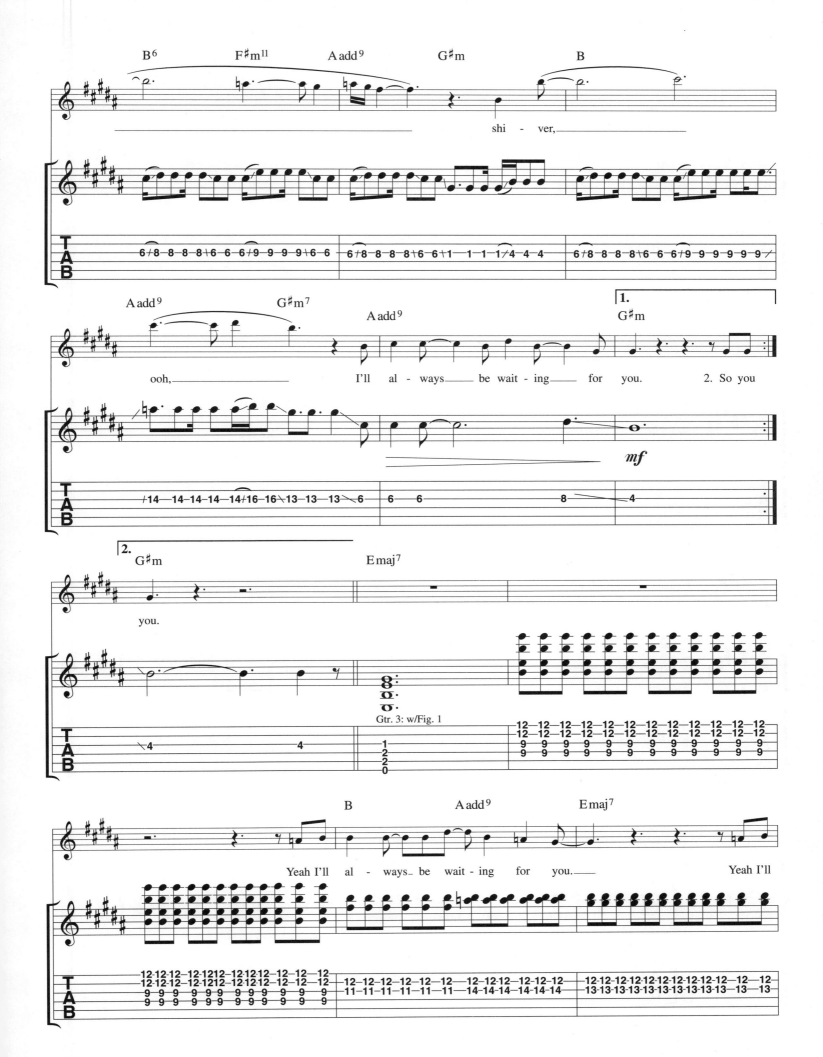

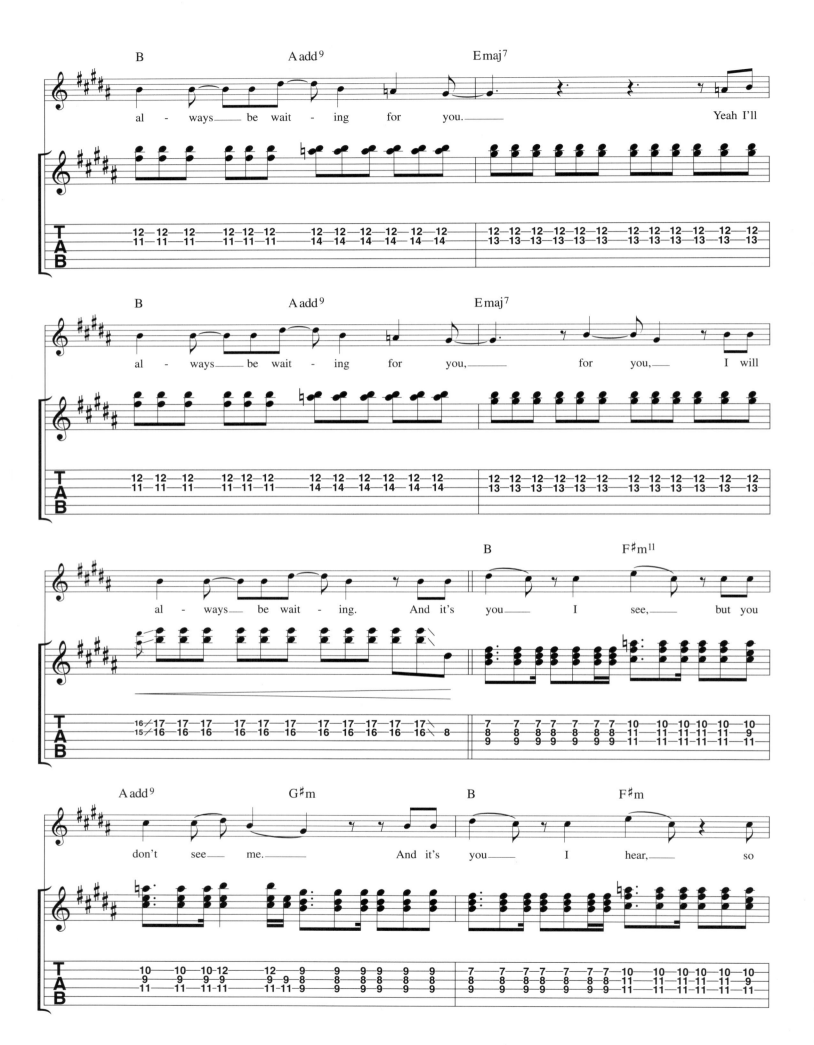

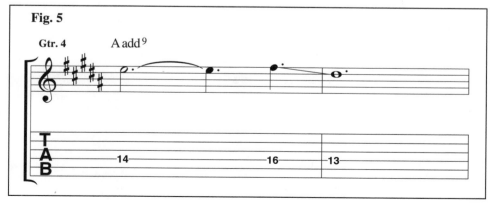

SPIES

Words & Music by Guy Berryman, Jon Buckland, Will Champion & Chris Martin

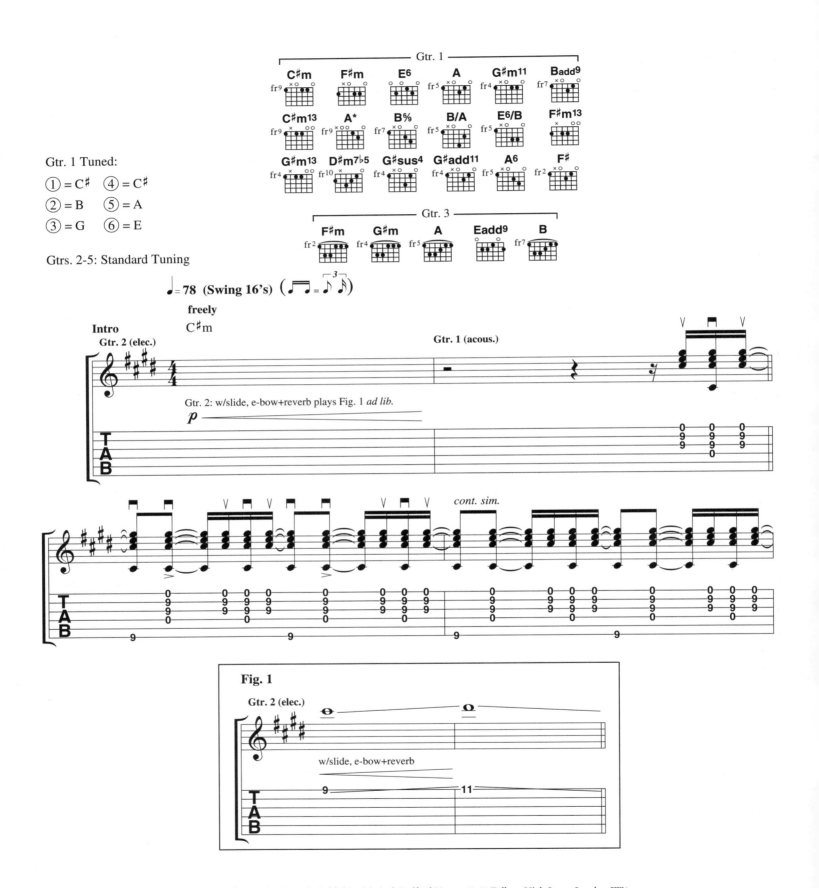

Verse F#m E⁶

(1.) I a-wake to find no peace of mind, I said, "How do
(2.) I a-wake to see that no - one is free,

2° Gtr. 3: w/Fig. 3 (x2)
Gtr. 2: tacet

A G#m¹¹

you live as a fu - gi - tive?" Down
- gi - tives, look at the way we live. Down

Fig. 3

Gtr. 3 (elec.) F#m Eadd⁹ A G#m

w/slight dist. + tremolo

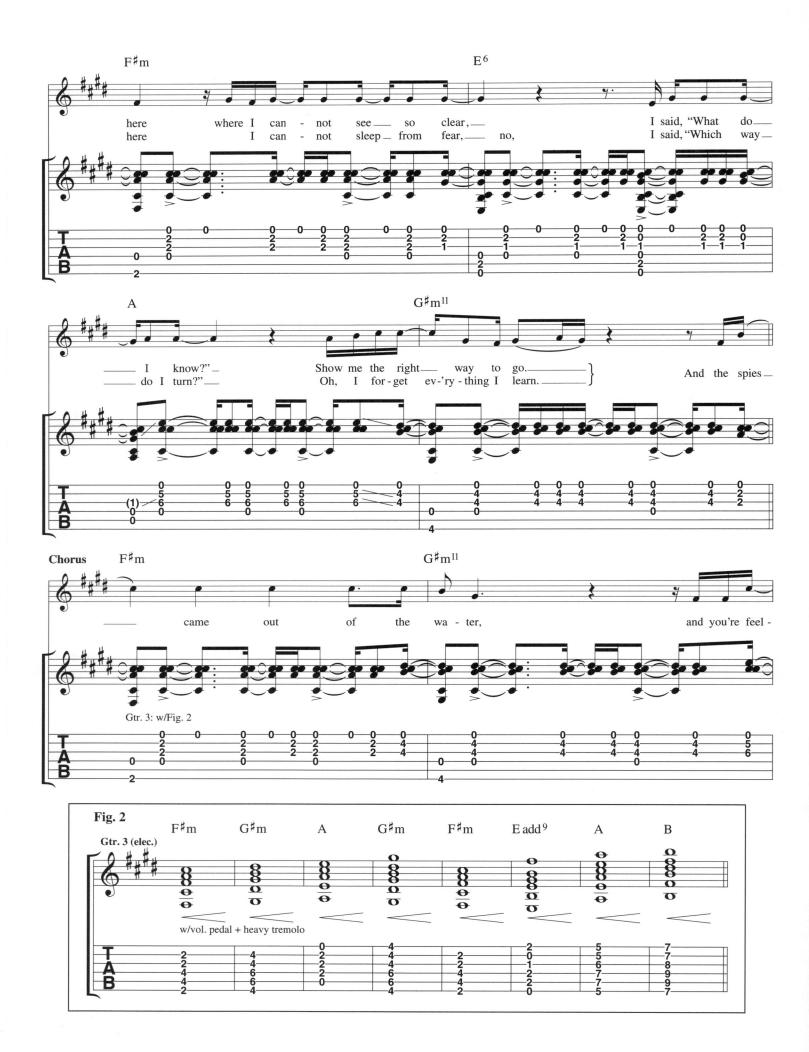

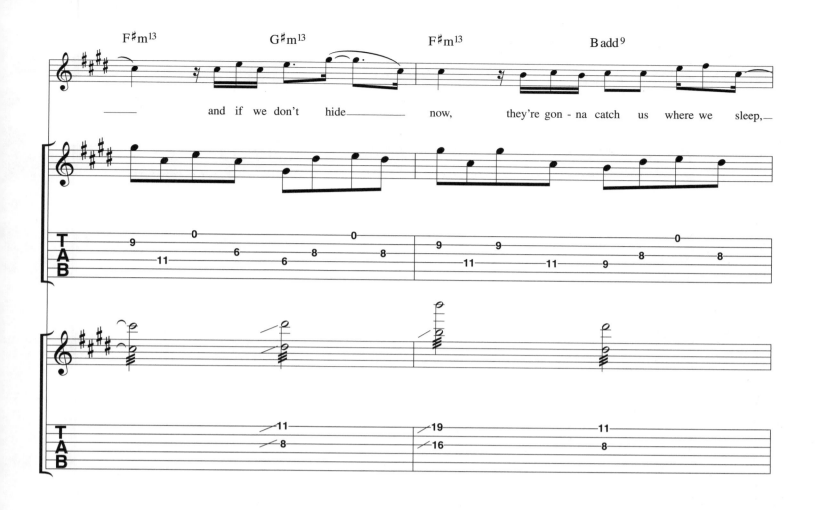

and if we don't hide_____ now, they're gon-na catch us where we sleep,_____

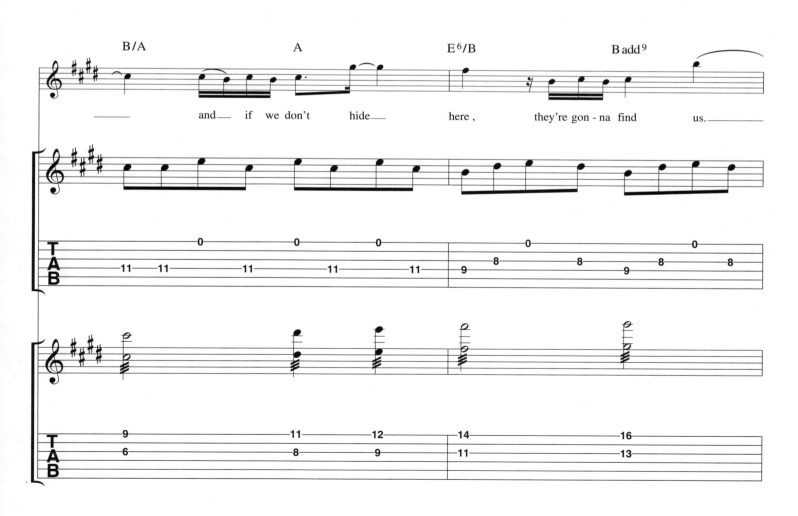

and_____ if we don't hide_____ here, they're gon-na find us._____

Chorus

Spies came out of the wa - ter, and you're feel-

- ing— so— good, 'cause you know— that those

Gtr. 3: w/Fig. 4

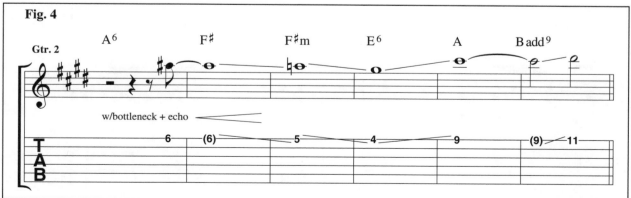

Fig. 4

Gtr. 2

w/bottleneck + echo

spies   hide   out   in e - ve - ry   cor - ner,   and they can't   touch—

you,   no,   'cause they're   just   spies.—

Outro

They're   just   spies.—

Play 4 times

SPARKS

Words & Music by Guy Berryman, Jon Buckland, Will Champion & Chris Martin

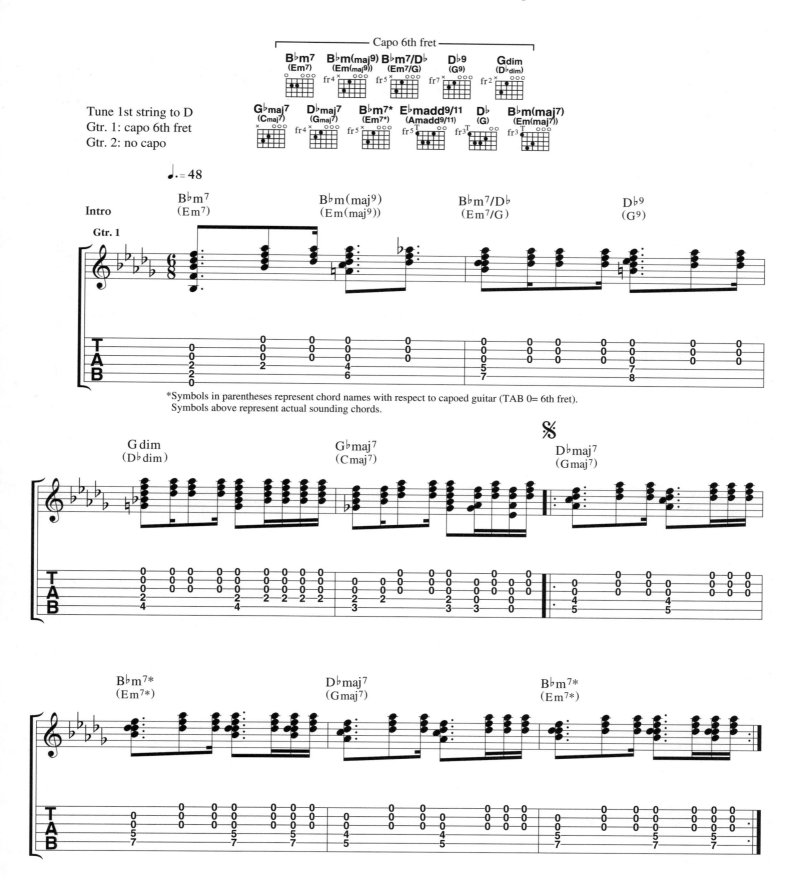

*Symbols in parentheses represent chord names with respect to capoed guitar (TAB 0= 6th fret).
Symbols above represent actual sounding chords.

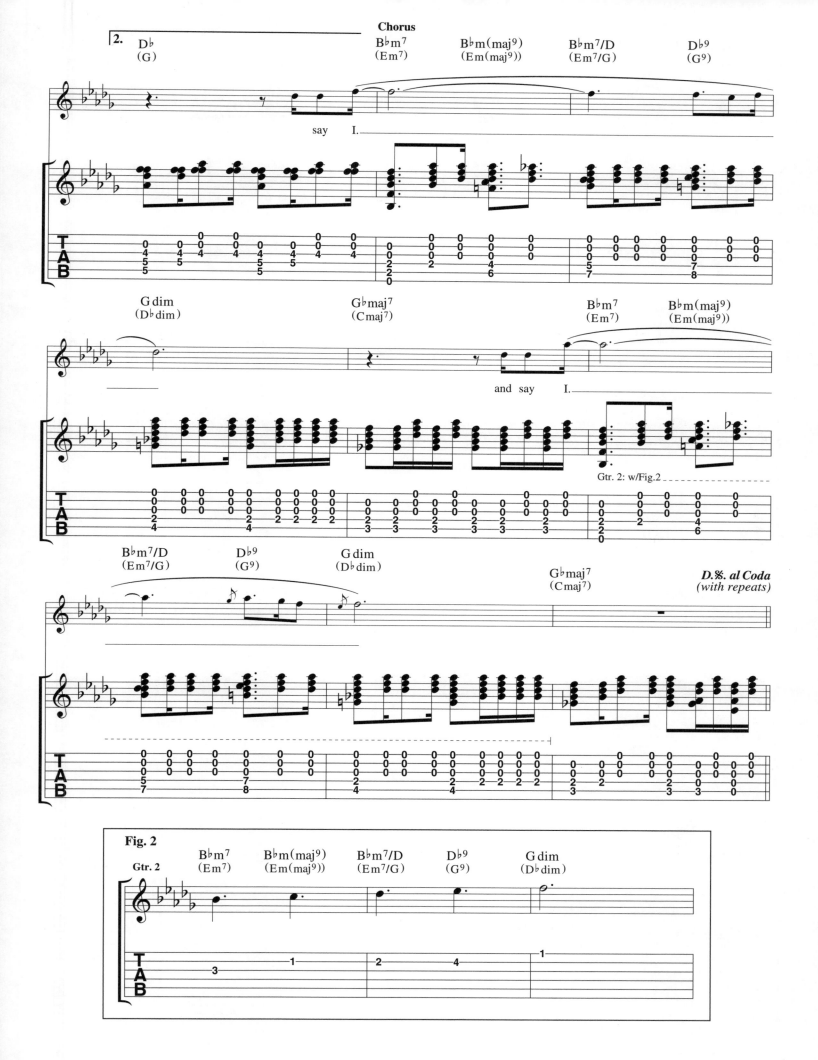

YELLOW

Words & Music by Guy Berryman, Jon Buckland, Will Champion & Chris Martin

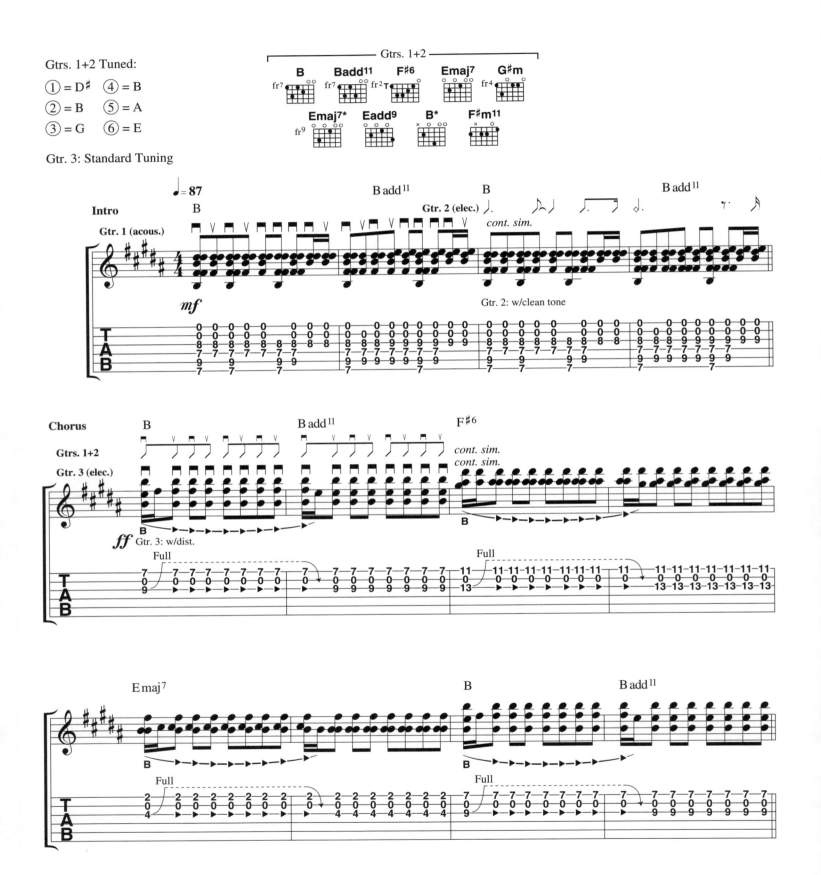

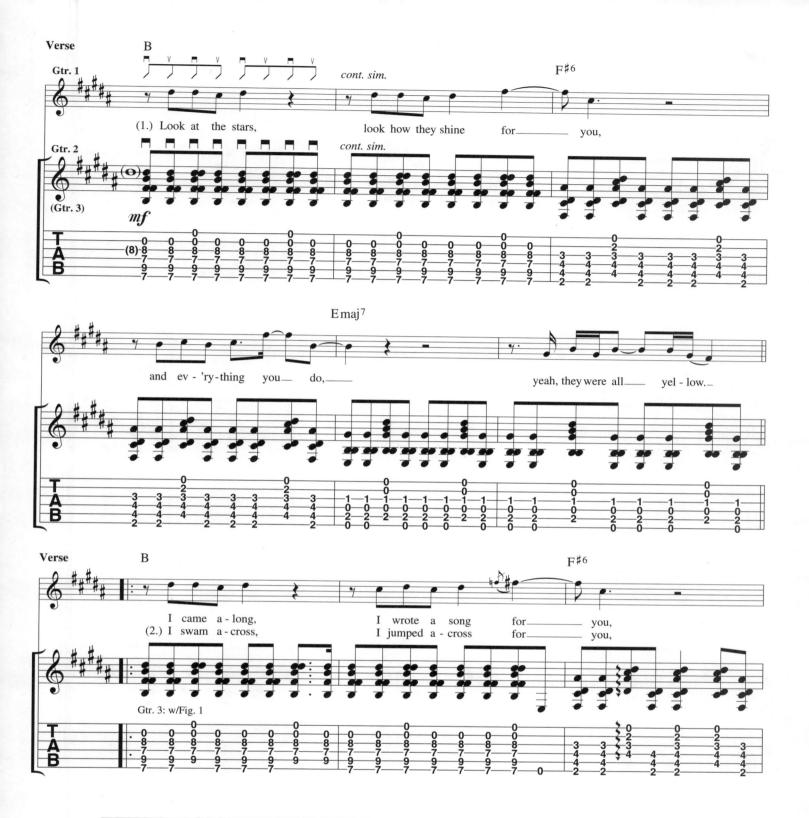

Verse

Gtr. 1 / Gtr. 2 / (Gtr. 3)

(1.) Look at the stars, look how they shine for_____ you,

and ev-'ry-thing you___ do,_____ yeah, they were all___ yel-low.__

Verse

I came a-long, I wrote a song for_____ you,
(2.) I swam a-cross, I jumped a-cross for_____ you,

Gtr. 3: w/Fig. 1

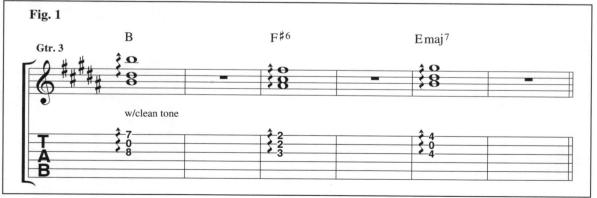

Fig. 1

Gtr. 3

w/clean tone

Emaj⁷

and all the things you___ do,___
oh, what a thing to___ do,___

B

and it was called___ yel - low.___
'cause you were all___ yel - low.___ I drew a line,

Gtr. 3: w/Fig. 1

B add¹¹

So then I took my___ turn,
I drew a line for___ you,

F♯⁶

Emaj⁷

oh, what a thing to've done,___
oh, what a thing to do,___

and it was all___ yel - low.___
and it was all___ yel - low.

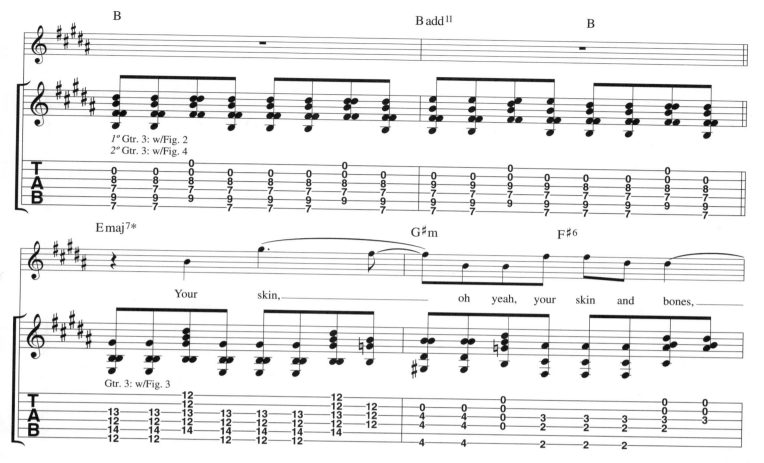

Your skin,_____ oh yeah, your skin and bones,_____

TROUBLE

Words & Music by Guy Berryman, Jon Buckland, Will Champion & Chris Martin

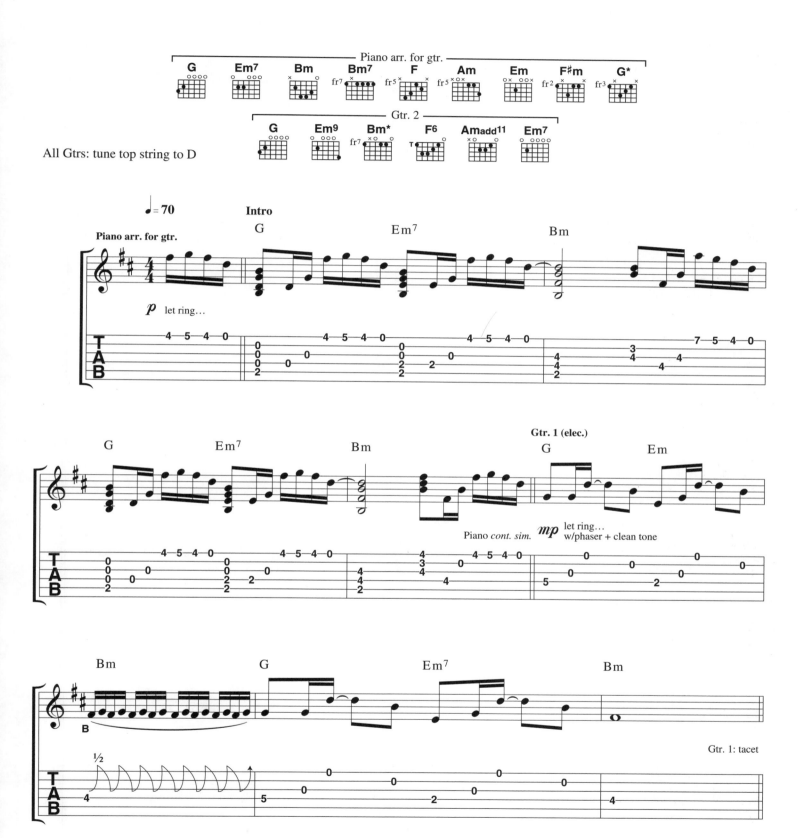

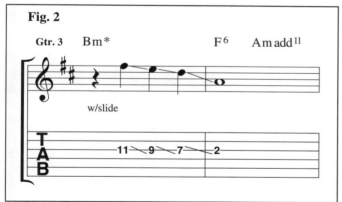

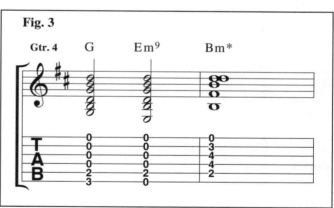

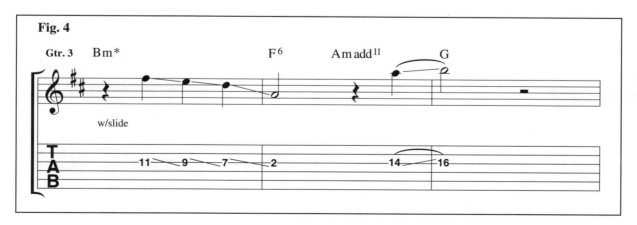

Bridge

And they spun a web____ for me,____ and they____ spun a web____ for me,____

Piano arr. for gtr.

____ and they____ spun a web____ for me.____

43

PARACHUTES

Words & Music by Guy Berryman, Jon Buckland, Will Champion & Chris Martin

WE NEVER CHANGE

Words & Music by Guy Berryman, Jon Buckland, Will Champion & Chris Martin

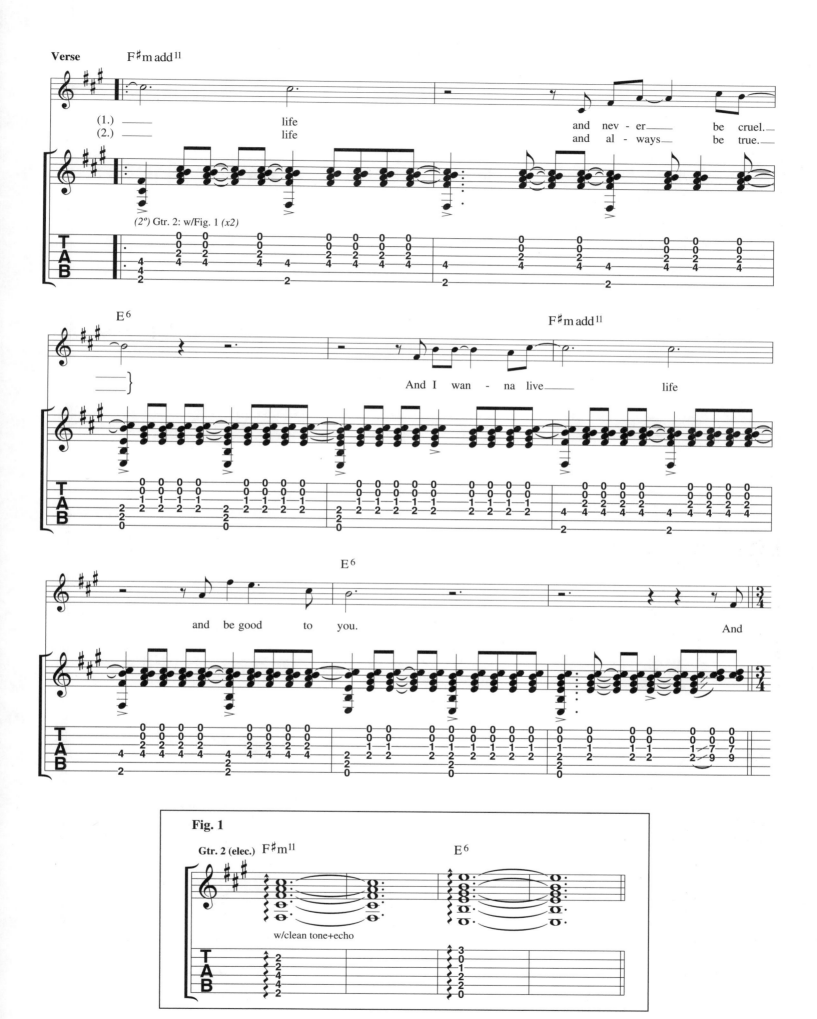

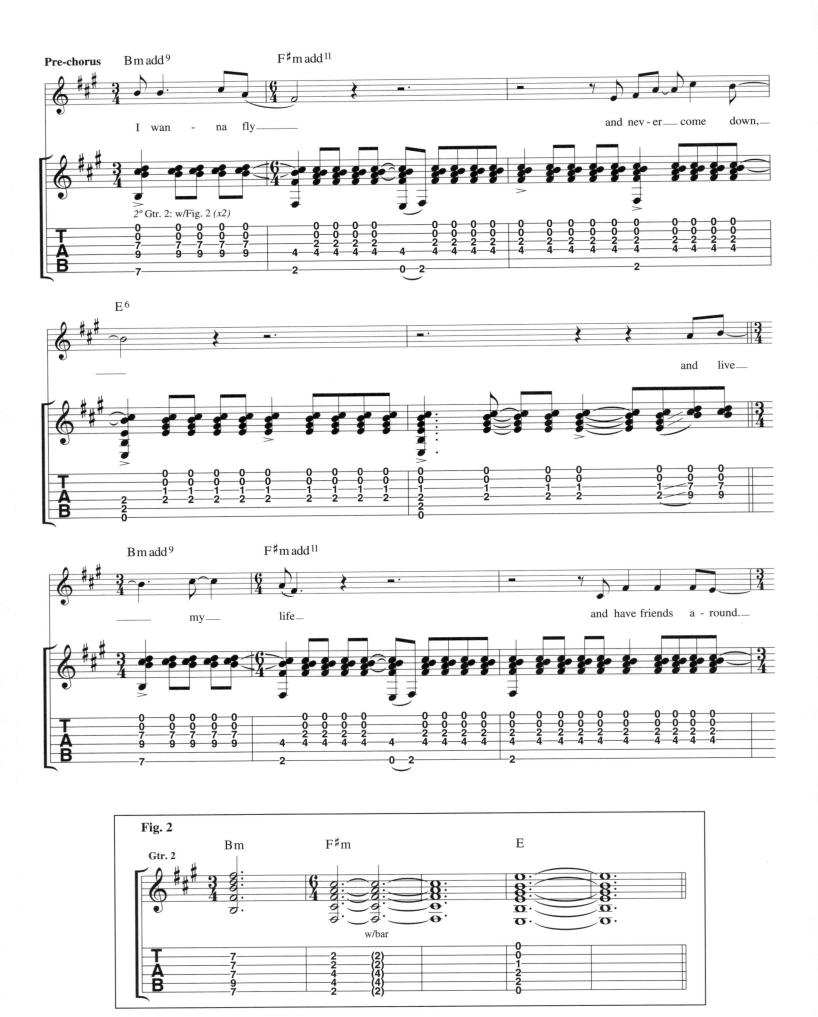

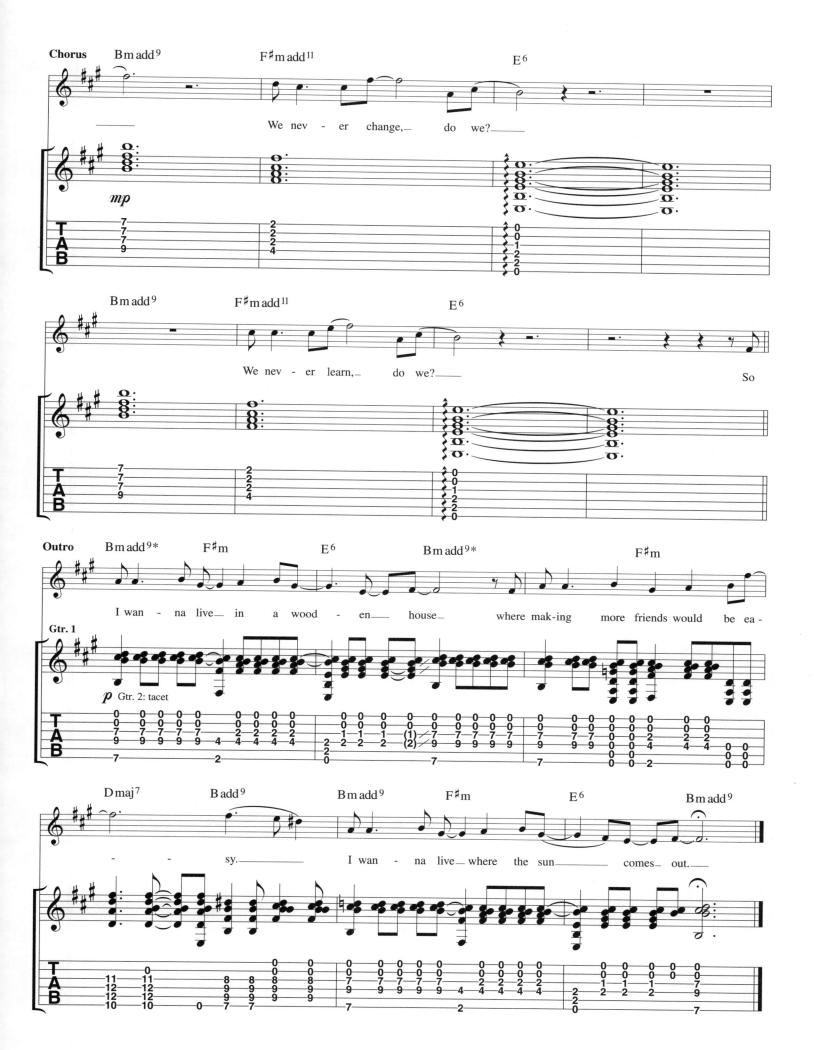

HIGH SPEED

Words & Music by Guy Berryman, Jon Buckland, Will Champion & Chris Martin

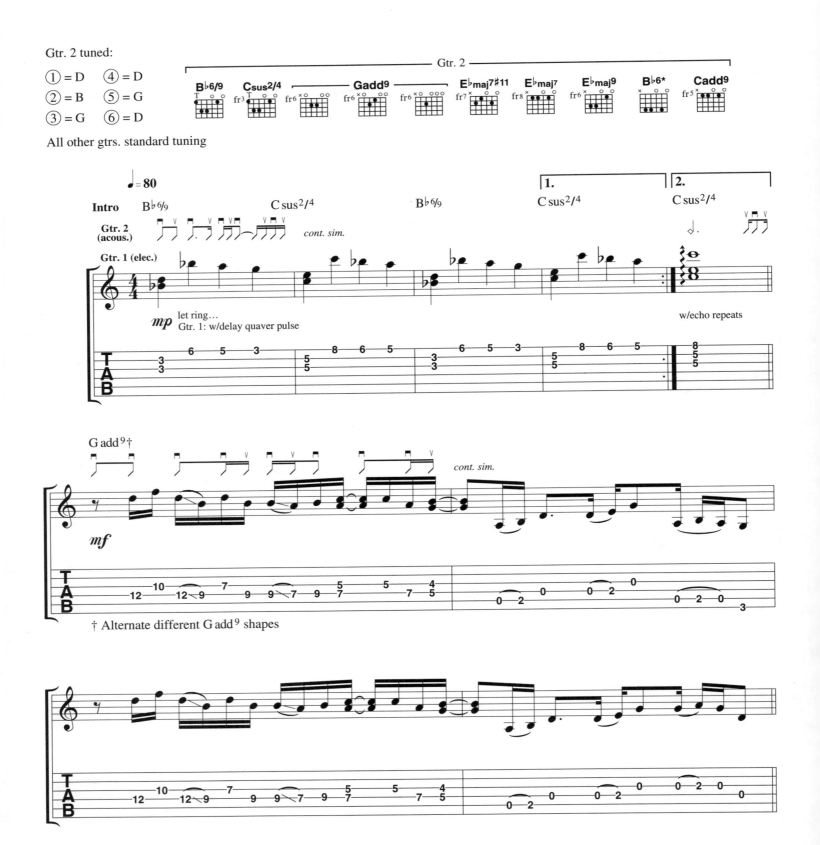

Verse

Can a-ny-bo-dy fly____ this thing?____
Can a-ny-bo-dy stop____ this thing?____

Be-fore my head ex-plodes,____ be-fore my head starts____ to ring.

We've been liv-ing a life

in - side a bub-ble.

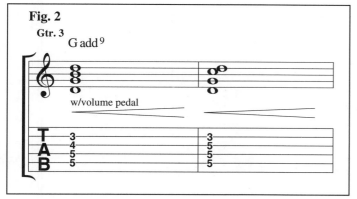

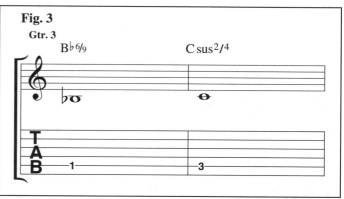

EVERYTHING'S NOT LOST

Words & Music by Guy Berryman, Jon Buckland, Will Champion & Chris Martin

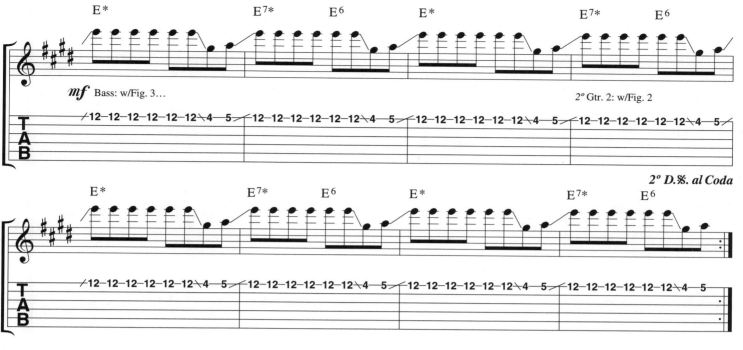

2° D.%. al Coda

lost.— Sing-ing out ah, ah, ah, yeah,— ah, ah, yeah,—
so come on yeah,— ah, ah, yeah,—

Piano arr. for gtr.

let ring…

Fig. 3

Bass

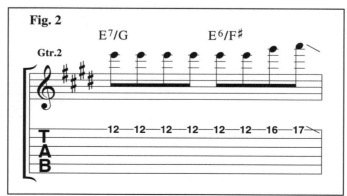

Fig. 2

Gtr.2

LIFE IS FOR LIVING

Words & Music by Guy Berryman, Jon Buckland, Will Champion & Chris Martin

then I don't let it stand in our way.

and I don't want to live it a - lone.

2. Cos

Sing ah.

Sing ah.

cont. sim.

And you sing ah.

2/04 (50099)